Taking the Fear out of interviews

A practical guide for interviewees

www.careerlifestylechoices.com

Marilyn Black

Copyright©Marilyn Black 2017

(Revision 2) written by Marilyn Black (Farmanfarmai), Panorama Consulting www.panoramaconsulting.co.uk. CareerLifestyleChoices is a trading name of Panorama Consulting.

All rights reserved. Except for the use in any review, the reproduction or utilisation of this work in whole or in part in any form by any electronic, mechanical or other means is not permitted without prior permission of the author.

The information provided in this document is my opinion only. My recommendations are based on experience and knowledge but there is no guarantee that as a result of reading this document or following the exercises, anyone will be successful in finding work, or more comfortable at interview, as many factors can affect the outcome.

Where links have been provided to Third Parties, Marilyn Black (Farmanfarmai), Panorama Consulting, has no liability for any actions taken, or advice given, by these companies or their representatives. These links are current at the time of going to press.

Contents

Why I Wrote This Book 1

About the Author 3

Putting 'Fear' in its Place 5

    Before the Day 5

    On the Day 11

The Tools Interviewers May Use and Why 14

    Psychometrics 14

    Competency-based Interviews 17

    Scenarios and Role Plays 19

    Telephone Interviews 20

    Panel Interviews 20

    Group Interviews 21

    Assessment Centres 21

The Tools You Can Use and Why 23

    Your CV 23

    Self-Image 28

    First Impressions 29

    Attitude 29

    Communicating Effectively 31

Targeting Your Job Search   34

Identifying your Strengths   34
Identifying your Personal Values   36
Identifying your Skills and Achievements   38
Identifying Potential Roles and Companies   40

Getting into Action   42

Have a Goal   42
Treat your Job Search like a Project   42
Be your Own Boss until you find another one   44
Making Friends with the Agencies   45
Speculative Approaches   47
Networking   48
Job Application Letters and Emails   49

What You Can Legally Expect   51

Employment Law Discriminations   51
Information Commissioner's Office (ICO)   52

Let's Practise   54

Competency-based Interview Questions   54

Why I Wrote This Book

As a Recruitment Consultant for many years, I saw first-hand the pain that numerous candidates experienced when looking for their first job or when changing careers. However, key challenges could have been avoided if they had been more aware of what to expect.

According to the Office for National Statistics (ONS), in April 2016 the unemployment rate for the whole UK was 5.0%, with 1.67 million people out of work. For the period Feb-Apr 2016 nearly 1 million people had been out of work, or actively seeking work, for up to 6 months. For the same period, youth unemployment (16 - 24 year olds) was 13.6% with 621,000 young people actively seeking work (including 216,000 full-time students seeking part-time work)

This unemployment rate and the level of people wishing to work longer, means that there is significant competition when people do apply for jobs. Moreover, although job satisfaction is not particularly high, many people in employment are reluctant to change companies due to the current uncertainty, putting further pressure on the job market.

Of course, if you are entirely satisfied with your career, some aspects of this book, such as the job search tips, are not for you. The interview preparation techniques, however, are equally relevant to promotional opportunities as they are to roles within another employer.

Looking for a new job because you are out of work or because you are feeling unfulfilled where you are, can affect confidence and make the whole process rather daunting.

The main purpose in writing this book is to take the mystery out of some interviewing techniques which you are likely to encounter and to provide a straightforward framework for you to follow until you have found work of your choice.

There is an abundance of information on the internet, so I have tried to focus on practical tips wherever I can to show you the "how" as well as the "what".

About the Author

I was introduced to the recruitment industry when it was in its infancy. Like many others at the time, I went to an agency for them to find me a job. As luck would have it, my face fitted and they offered me the opportunity to train with them as a recruitment consultant.

Fast-forward 30+ years and I've experienced 'ups and downs' like anyone else. I've worked for corporates, I've worked for myself, I've experienced recessions and the following 'booms' but above all I have been lucky to be in a business where there is constant change.

I have been an independent consultant now for 14 years having experienced redundancy during an industry downturn. Obviously this was not planned and it came at a particularly bad time but when is the timing right for redundancy?

Overall, I did look upon it as an opportunity rather than a threat but I remember all too well that there were some really difficult days. Getting the mind and body back into gear isn't easy and if you are in a similar situation - I know how you feel!

Whilst I draw mostly from my personal and business experience, I am also accredited in (CEB) Saville & Holdsworth Ability Testing and Psychometric /Personality Profiling and Strengthscope™ assessment tools.

My soapbox moment comes when I am thinking, or talking, about people being able to be in control of their own lives. Current forecasts are that it will become the norm to live to 100, and we will need to work past present retirement age or supplement our earnings in some way.

Marilyn Black

I, therefore, wish to help people create the best career and lifestyle choices for them, whether they are employed or working for themselves.

Please visit my website www.careerlifestylechoices.com for an overview.

If you feel that I can help you in any way please email me: marilyn@careerlifestylechoices.com and I will respond within 24 hours - most likely sooner.

Putting 'Fear' in its Place

I've heard that 'public speaking' rates very close to 'death' when people have been asked what they fear most. I have, however, seen many candidates who are so nervous before, during and after an interview that I would also rate 'interviews' up high on the list.

Really, it gets down to fear of the unknown, the feeling that you are being judged by people you don't know and that you will have difficulty answering their questions.

Being well prepared will remove these worries so that you can be relaxed during the interview and do yourself justice ... believe me, it works.

Before the Day

Obviously, the more you can do before the day, the better. Whatever happens, don't go into an interview and think that you can 'wing it'. It rarely works and besides, you are likely to have put in a fair amount of effort into getting to interview stage, so don't waste it.

Follow this checklist and it should help greatly:

Research the company.

> Write a list of the potential questions as they come to mind, and then choose the top 3-5 that are the most relevant. If there are more, then that is fine, but they must be specific and relevant.

The internet has a wealth of information so explore the company and market sector in depth. By doing this, you should have no shortage of potential questions that you can ask at interview. It will also help you determine if the company is going to be right for you. Look further than just their website, check out forums and competitors and go as wide and deep as you can.

Research the interviewer.

It is likely that you will be told the name of the interviewer(s) before the date. If you are not told, then it is quite in order for you to ask the company or the agency. If they are unable to tell you prior to the interview, just accept it as sometimes interviewers can be decided at the last minute.

If you do have a name, then finding out a little about them beforehand sometimes helps to make them more real and not just a job title. Social media is an ideal source for this, such as **LinkedIn** and **Facebook**.

Ask about the interview process

Get as much information as you can regarding the interview process beforehand so that you know exactly what to expect. Forewarned is definitely forearmed and it will significantly reduce your stress level. Companies and agencies are more than likely to offer this but if not, ask. They will think more of you for doing so.

Write down three key reasons why you think the job to which you are applying is necessary to the company's management.

It helps to give some thought as to why a company may be recruiting. Essentially commercial companies aim to run profitably by increasing sales and managing costs. All organisations, whether private or public, have a reason for existing and job advertisements will reflect a specific need that they have to resolve a problem. For instance, they may be seeking an effective manager with strong leadership skills to take their business to the next level. In this example, a problem could be low morale in the team or it could be that

Taking the Fear Out of Interviews

they need to have a more dynamic sales focus or something else. You are not necessarily going to be able to know for sure before you attend an interview but just thinking about the possibilities could help you ask some very relevant questions.

Imagine you are a manager recruiting for this role. Consider not only the key functions of the job but also where it might impact other people and departments.

Marilyn Black

<u>Write down three key reasons why you are applying for the role and what you can offer.</u>

You are likely to be asked this question at interview and if you enthusiastically demonstrate that there is a good match between the job, your skills and what you are looking for in the future, the interviewer should be impressed. At the very least you will have shown that you have given their opportunity serious thought and are not just treating it as one of a number.

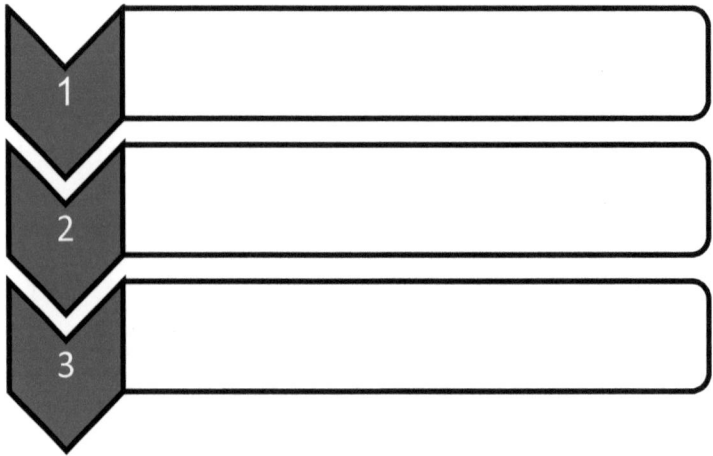

Prepare a 30 - 45 sec summary.

Many interviewers will kick-off with a rapport-building opener, such as "Please tell me little about yourself". Always be respectful of the interviewer's time and the time allocated to your interview.

If you have prepared a quick verbal summary of the following then you will be answering that question fluently and succinctly. It is often good to include some non- work related interest or passion so that the interviewer can see what motivates and enthuses you.

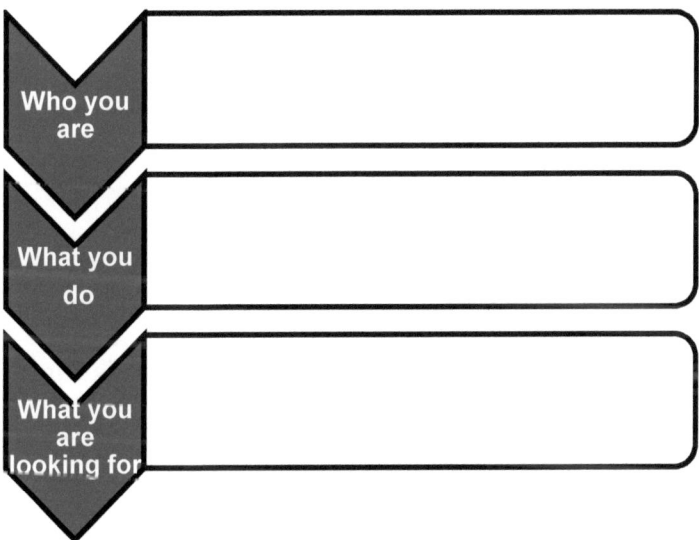

It really is important to keep it brief as the interviewer will either become bored or irritated that you have overlooked the fact you were asked to tell him/her "a little".

Marilyn Black

Practise answering some hypothetical interview questions.

I will be covering the more specific Competency-based interview questions in the next section with some examples in 'Let's Practise'.

Here are a few examples of generic questions but if you read the job advertisement carefully, you can get a very good idea of the questions you might be asked.

> What are your career goals for the next five years?
>
> What do you consider to be your strengths?
>
> Where would you say you need to develop your experience?
>
> What are your interests outside of work?
>
> How do you think your current team members would describe you?
>
> How do you think your manager would describe you?
>
> What motivates you to put in your greatest effort?
>
> What interests you about our product or service?
>
> What is your understanding of the role at this time?
>
> What are the two or three important things that you are looking for from this job?

On the Day

Remember the 40/5 rule.

There is nothing worse than arriving late for an interview, unless it is completely unavoidable, of course. Assuming that there are no reasons for being delayed, then aim to arrive 40 mins before the interview time. This should give you time to park the car or walk/taxi from the station, depending on the circumstances. The plan is to time it so that you are walking into reception 5 mins before you are due.

If, for some reason beyond your control, you believe you are likely to arrive late, then inform the company as soon as you can so that you are not getting stressed before arriving. They may decide it is best to reschedule.

Interviewers may be inexperienced.

Whilst it is normal to assume interviewers are sufficiently trained and will ask searching questions, the reality is that interviewers are sometimes less experienced than you might think. For instance, if you are being interviewed by a Line Manager or Team Leader then their primary role is to meet their business objectives, project deadlines etc and their exposure to interviewing may be limited. Having said that, larger companies normally have a formal interview process supported by a Human Resources team which should ensure all interviewers meet the required standard.

The interviewer may follow a structured format.

If so, it is likely at the end of the interview that you will be asked if there is anything else you would like to add regarding your suitability for the role. Take advantage of this – but keep it concise and relevant.

If you are not asked and you feel that some areas of your experience have been overlooked, then offer the information anyway - when you have left the room it will be too late!

What are they looking for?

I will be covering personal attributes in a following chapter, so this is a checklist regarding content only:

Answer questions fully but concisely - talking too much is often a sign of nervousness so try to avoid it.

Knowledge of the company and industry sector.

Keen interest in the specific job.

Evidence that your skills, experience and competencies meet their criteria. This will be obtained by interview questions and possibly some test or assessment. It is always a good idea to take along reports or anything similar which demonstrate your abilities. More detail regarding testing and assessment are in the next chapter.

An understanding of your own development needs. Successful candidates rarely tick all the boxes regarding skills and experience. If they do then an interviewer may have concern regarding how long the candidate would remain interested or motivated. It is much more likely for there to be some development needs where training may be required or where there is scope for you to enhance your potential. If you can say what you think these may be, then the interviewer will be impressed because you are demonstrating that you are looking for personal development.

An appreciation of your character. The interviewer will be considering how you are likely to interact with the rest of the team, management, customers etc, depending on the role. So your hobbies, interests or other life experiences may also be discussed.

Positivity. It is never a good idea to criticise past or present employers, however justified you believe it may be. If you have had bad experiences then try to see the positives, such as lessons you may have learnt.

<u>The easier you make it for them, the easier it will be.</u>

A quick summary, of how to get the best out of an interview:

Respect their time. Interviews typically last 1-1.5 hours and the interviewer may well have several people to interview that day.

Be responsive and concise when answering their questions.

Read the signs. Is the interviewer relaxed and smiling or getting restless?

Go prepared with a few well thought out questions about the company, the role and future development.

Practise interview questions so that you can answer fluently.

Be honest. If you don't know something, it is much better to say so rather than try and bluff. The interviewer will respect your honesty.

Remember an interview is a two-way process - this helps to boost confidence and it introduces some balance into the discussion.

Relax - ultimately, it is just a job. I know that sometimes getting a particular job seems vital at the time but it is important to keep it in perspective. Having this mindset, will help you get the best out of the interview process and will project you in the best light.

Marilyn Black

The Tools Interviewers May Use and Why

Getting to interview stage should boost confidence and self-esteem, if this is lacking, as it is confirmation that your experience will have met the company's selection criteria to some degree. It is worth bearing in mind that today the majority of interviewers will be assessing not only experience and knowledge but also the softer skills, such as communication and team playing. This is the age of the service and information industries and even the most technical roles are likely now to need the ability to interact effectively with others.

Interviews have become less subjective and can no longer rely on 'gut feeling'. Now, various tools are applied to assess whether you actually have the required level of experience and appropriate personality traits for the role.

This list is not exhaustive but is an overview of what you might expect.

Psychometrics

Psychometric Assessments are widely used by Human Resource professionals to bring objectivity into the recruitment or development process.

> **Top Tips for Ability Tests**
> - **Work as quickly as possible** - applies to both online or manual testing.
> - Be mindful of the **time allocation**.
> - You should get **practice questions**.
> - You are likely **NOT** to complete all the questions
> - There **ARE** right and wrong answers

Whilst there are numerous assessments available, psychometrics typically measure

Aptitude/Ability or Personality Traits. It is normal for companies to inform candidates of any testing or assessments prior to interview. The following examples are based on the CEB Saville & Holdsworth (SHL) range of psychometric products as this is where my personal experience lies. SHL has been prominent in workplace psychometrics for over twenty years.

Examples of SHL Assessments:

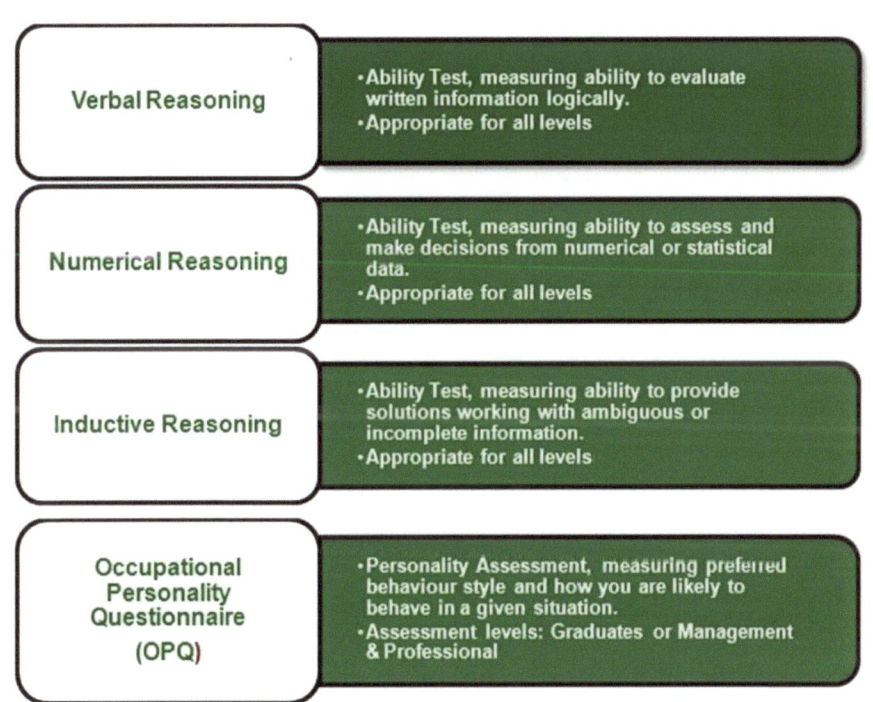

FREE Practice SHL Ability Tests and the Personality Questionnaires

are available on this link: **https://www.cebglobal.com/shldirect/index.php/en.** Having completed your registration and the test of your choice, the results will be emailed directly to you by SHL but come back to me if you have any questions. (Disclaimer: Please be aware that whilst I am accredited in the tests and personality questionnaires mentioned above, I do not have an affiliate relationship with SHL and therefore do not financially benefit by you visiting their website through this link)

Strengthscope ™

Another psychometric that does what it says on the tin. It assesses your natural talents and whether you are using them effectively in the workplace. This is widely used for career development purposes but is becoming more popular as a recruiting tool, so you may come across it. Essentially, there is evidence that when people are able to apply their natural strengths fully in the workplace, there is a very positive impact on performance. No practice tests are available but more information can be found on my website www.careerlifestylechoices.com.

Online Assessments

Nowadays, online assessments are popular with employers and candidates, primarily due to time efficiency. For example, if you are selected for interview from your CV and if the company uses psychometrics as part of their selection process, then you are likely to receive a link to an online provider prior to the interview.

The benefit of this is that you can complete the assessment in your own time with no distractions. Some people are concerned that results can be manipulated as the assessment is unsupervised but this is highly unlikely due to their mathematical design.

> **Top Tips**
> **Personality Assessments**
>
> - **There ARE NO "right or wrong" answers** - the selectors are looking for a cultural fit - respond with your most natural answer as quickly as possible.
> - **Be honest** - don't look for the "desired" answer as this will be evident to the assessor
> - **Don't worry** if the questions are repetitive
> - **Results** should be discussed at interview

All of the above assessments can be conducted either on paper or online. At interview you should receive feedback and the assessment report may be used as a basis for the interview questions.

It is worth asking the company or recruitment agency before the day whether there are assessments. If there are, then it is perfectly in order to ask which one(s) and research them on the internet.

Competency-based Interviews

In my experience, the knowledge that an interview will be competency-based creates another 'fear trigger' because people don't always know what to expect. Competency-based questions, however, exist so that the interviewer can assess your actual experience and judge if it meets the selection criteria for the role. It is important for companies to take the guess work out of the interview process and interviewers can no longer rely on 'gut feeling'. Decisions can be challenged by a candidate so having documented evidence to support a decision is not only wise but also a legal requirement. Whatever format the interview takes, you will be entitled to feedback. When a company creates a job description, behavioural competencies will be included.

Here are some examples of behavioural competencies:

Thinking
- Attention to Detail
- Creativity
- Planning & Organisation
- Time Management

Delivery
- Decision Making & Judgement
- Flexibility
- Initiative
- Resilience
- Strategic Awareness

Relational
- Developing Others
- Empathy
- Influencing
- Leadership
- Managing & Controlling
- Relationship Management
- Teamwork

> Examples of Competency-based interview questions and recommendations for answering them are in Let's Practise

Scenarios and Role Plays

Ability tests, Psychometric Assessments /Personality Profiles and Competency-based interview techniques can be applied to any job level.

To give a deeper layer of understanding and assessment for specialist or management roles, companies may include Scenarios and Role Plays in their assessment process, more often in an Assessment Centre situation.

Scenarios and Role Plays are based on real life, workplace situations and assess how a candidate is likely to handle them. Scenario questionnaires can be done online via an assessment provider prior to attending the Assessment Centre although some companies create their own for closer alignment with a specific role.

> Prepare for Role Plays by practising typical situations beforehand with a friend

It has to be said that Role Plays are often uncomfortable for the interviewer as well as the candidate as it is difficult to be natural. Role Plays generally take place in an Assessment Centre situation so you are likely to be informed before the day and can prepare well.

Telephone Interviews

> **Telephone Interviews Top Tips**
> - Be ready at least 5 minutes before the call.
> - Take the call in a quiet place where there can be no interruptions
> - Have your CV in front of you
> - Have the Job Description or Job Advertisement in front of you.
> - Be aware that the interviewer will be assessing how you communicate, so answer as fluently as you can.

Telephone interviews are normally the first stage of the interview process, following receipt of your CV. They may vary in length and detail but this first level screening should not be underestimated. In addition to job related questions the interviewer will also clarify other essential criteria.

Panel Interviews

It is quite normal to have two interviewers at the same time, particularly with the larger companies. It is wise to anticipate this and a typical situation would be for a Line Manager and HR Professional to split the interview between job related and behavioural competency questions. Alternatively, another typical example would be the first interview by a Line Manager and Team Leader for job related questions followed by the HR interview. However, there are a variety of options. If you have applied for a senior position, then you may well be interviewed by a panel which typically would be 4-6 people comprising technical specialists, HR specialists and Line Managers but again, there is no standard. Whilst this can be intimidating it is more likely to be relaxed and informal as the interviewers will

> A key benefit of a panel interview is that there will be a consensus decision to hire which creates another layer of objectivity to the process.

probably be wishing to put you at ease. In addition to thorough preparation, try to be as relaxed as you can be on the day. When you are asked questions by one member of the panel, direct your answer to everyone so that the atmosphere is conversational and inclusive.

Group Interviews

Sometimes, if recruiting for a number of roles, companies may invite you in for a Group Interview where you will meet the other candidates which, in this respect, is the same as an Assessment Centre. Where it might vary is that psychometrics and other assessment tools may not necessarily be used at this stage.

In any Group situation, your aim should be to stand out from the crowd in a positive way. Following the Before the Day tips will help you create a good first impression and be appropriately prepared. Some people in this situation become very assertive and talk over the other candidates. Be aware that at all times the interviewers will be seeing how you interact with others and will envisage how you might act in a business situation, such as with team members or with customers. They will be looking for politeness and the ability to put your point across in a non-aggressive way.

Assessment Centres

Where there is larger scale recruitment, you may be asked to attend an Assessment Centre where your experience and personality will be assessed over a few hours or days in a group environment. The benefit of this style of recruitment to the company is that assessing over time can give them an understanding of consistent ability.

Marilyn Black

Whilst it might seem scary at first, the benefit to you would be that you have time to make a great impression and also have the opportunity to judge if the company will suit you. An Assessment Centre will vary according to the company but typically can include psychometric assessments, scenarios, role plays, group discussions, case studies, presentations and one-to-one interviews.

The Tools You Can Use and Why

Your CV

Your Curriculum Vitae/Resume' is your door opener and therefore an extremely important marketing tool. You should treat it with the respect it deserves and create content which is going to demonstrate the relevance of your experience to the role and create a sense of your personality. It is a tough call but it is really worthwhile to spend time and create something that makes you proud. Often people are on automatic pilot where their work is concerned, particularly if they have been doing the same role or been employed by the same company for some time, but it is important to be as objective as you can without inflating your achievements or being too modest.

Top Tips for writing your CV

Always put yourself in the place of the CV reviewer or interviewer. They will only have a limited time to decide if your CV qualifies you for an interview, so keep it brief and relevant. Two pages is a good guide, no more than three.

Bear in mind that they will be looking for answers to **four key questions:**

What do you want to do?

Why are you qualified to do it?

How well have you done it?

Where have you done it?

What do you want to do? Your Profile will be at the top of your CV. Be very clear about what you are looking for from the role. Change it as necessary for different roles and employers so that your objective is clear and focused. The CV reviewer will not wish to guess and may just reject your application at the first stage.

Why are you qualified to do it? Using bullet points provide a Summary of why you are qualified to accomplish your objective. Put yourself in the reviewer's place again and think "Why should they hire me?"

How well have you done it? The Achievement section is vital and is appropriate regardless of your level of experience. All companies employ people to solve a problem of some nature. Achievement based CV's are, therefore, powerful as the prospective employer can see very quickly if your experience could resolve their specific problem based on past experience. Perhaps you are thinking that you did not achieve very much but, even if you did not achieve all objectives, think of the value you did provide. Think of the times you were given positive feedback and encouragement, earned promotions and made contributions. Perhaps you saved the company money or helped team members with challenges. Think as broadly as you can and make sure that your choice of words is dynamic, such as Achieved, Delivered, Promoted, Managed, Created etc...

Where have you done it? In the Experience section, state the companies where you have worked with the appropriate dates. It is best to write them in reverse chronological order and make sure there are no gaps. If you have not worked for a period, then say why. If you just leave a gap, it will raise a negative in the reviewer's mind so face it head on. The interviewer will be far more respectful of an honest CV and would be unlikely to trust ambiguity.

Education & Qualifications. List where you attended school and university and the qualifications you achieved. Include professional qualifications and memberships.

Finish off with **Personal Details & Interests** which should include nationality, marital status, current driving licence and key interests. Try and portray yourself as a well-rounded person. For instance, if you are a member of Rotary or Rotaract, this will show that you have a wide range of interests and a community spirit. Equally, if you are a graduate returning from a gap year abroad, this can show inner resourcefulness.

You should **not state your Age** on a CV and companies are no longer permitted to ask your age on an application form

Also just state **References by Request** rather than list your referees' contact details, otherwise they may regret offering if they receive too many requests!

There is no universal format for writing a CV, but it should be positive, concise, factual and give some insight to your character.

White paper, clear fonts and good layout are best. Try to avoid high colours and dramatic layout unless you are applying for a role in a very creative industry where it might be appreciated.

<u>An example of a CV layout is overleaf:</u>

Sample CV Layout

Your Name

Address
Email
Mobile

> Contact details can be included in Personal Details if preferred

Profile

> What do you want to do? 5-7 impact statements which basically describe your strengths and the type of role you are seeking. Use bold words and try to demonstrate energy and interest.

Summary

> Why are you qualified to do it? Bullet point statements showing how you are qualified for the role - *"Why should they hire me?"*

Achievements

> How well have you done it? High impact words describing your key achievements. Bullet point format

Experience Summary

(From - To)   Employer's Company Name

> In reverse chronological order, summarise your employer's business and your job role responsibilities. Do not leave gaps for any periods of unemployment - state reasons.

Education & Qualifications

> This could be included in personal details. Also, if particularly relevant to a role, move it to the first page.
>
> Include Professional Qualifications and Memberships here.

Personal Details & Interests

> Always include Nationality, Marital status, Driving Licence. Omit Age.

References on Request

Self-Image

Having a positive self-image is important as it has a direct impact on your confidence levels and general attitude. We all have life experiences which sometimes do not make us feel good about ourselves. A negative self-image could have been triggered in childhood resulting in a feeling of not being 'good enough'. Or it could be the result of some mistakes where guilt is still lingering. Everybody has 'ups and downs' but if you are due to attend an interview it is important to feel good about yourself.

> **An approach that may help**
>
> - **Reframe a negative experience into a positive one but still keeping it true.**
> - **Think about the specific challenges that you faced, what you learnt and any positives which resulted.**

Example 1:	Possible Reframe
You failed to deliver a project on time and are feeling guilty because you feel that you have let people down - your company, your team mates and your customers.	This is very unusual as I have a strong track record in delivering projects on time to budget. There were exceptional circumstances but the challenges gave me a greater understanding of the customer's needs and I now have an excellent opportunity to develop further business.

Example 2	Possible Reframe
You have applied for jobs for six months and have not been asked to attend an interview. You are feeling rejected and that you are not good enough.	I haven't been asked for interview yet but there is considerable competition. I will ask for feedback so that I target my applications better. Every day is a step closer to getting the right job.

First Impressions

First impressions do count, particularly when attending interviews. It is the **only** thing you can be judged on before the formal interview process starts. So be conscious from the earliest stage of a telephone call, an email application or submitting your CV that you are either creating a bad or a good impression.

Attitude

Having a positive attitude is vital whilst you job search and when you are working in your new job.

Easy to say, I hear you say ...

Yes, it starts with a positive self-image but even if you do not accomplish this, it is important to remember that people can only judge you on what they see and hear. So even if you are not feeling in a positive or upbeat mood, try to speak and act in a positive and likeable manner when you are with other people as this alone can change your mood.

It is worth bearing in mind that receptionists are people with thoughts, feelings and voices and are often asked by their managers how a candidate has acted whilst waiting for their appointment. I have interviewed candidates who could not be nicer or more professional when speaking to me but have been rude or offhand with someone they have not considered important - big mistake! It raises doubt in the interviewer's mind regarding how you are likely to interact with external customers or members of a team and is an unnecessary negative before to you start.

Sometimes people who are very experienced can feel uncomfortable when being interviewed by a younger person. This may be a result of the interviewer feeling unsure of their ground and possibly a little nervous due to your level of experience. It may be a result of some resentment on your part that the interviewer cannot possibly have the number of year's experience that you have! You can never guarantee if you are going to feel any rapport with the interviewer. You can, however, ensure that you create the best impression by mentally preparing yourself to have a healthy respect for any interviewer.

In my opinion, age consciousness is over-rated as I have interviewed 50 year olds with the mindset of someone in their 30's and graduates with attitudes of people much older. Age, these days, should not be a barrier or a qualification and is less important than being able to relate to people across all ages and at all levels.

If you have an honest, open-minded attitude and let people see the 'real' you, rapport can be established very quickly. Obviously, no-one relates to everyone all of the time; there will be some people with whom you can not relate to at all. Personally, I believe that most people, with a little effort and foresight, can relate to most people, but if you can't then accept it and move on.

Communicating Effectively

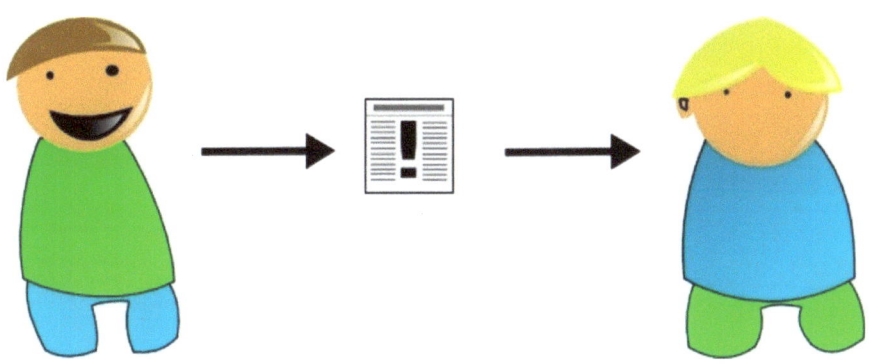

(photo source: Einar Faanes)

Being able to communicate effectively applies to all jobs at all levels. At one time, highly technical roles would treat interpersonal and communication skills as a lesser priority but that has more or less changed due to the shift of our workplace to a service culture.

Effective communication, however, can take a variety of forms ....

Written Communication

This can start with correct grammar in your CV and whether you have put across your experience in an interesting way. If you are being interviewed for a role which requires report writing then take along examples. Sometimes these can trigger discussion and be another way to really show that you have the experience for the job.

We all know that there are good and bad ways to write emails. As they are generally an informal method of communication, it's advisable to think twice before clicking the 'send' button. This is particularly important when you are working under pressure. It is usual now to apply for jobs via the internet and emails but I recommend you take the lead from the company with regard to an informal or more formal approach. If you have not had communication from them, then it is best to take the more formal approach in the first instance.

Verbal Communication

Whether you are on the telephone or at interview you should be conversational, rapport building and answering the questions concisely.

If you have been asked a challenging question it is far better to pause and think so that you can respond clearly and with impact. Resist the temptation to rush in with unstructured responses. This is one reason why practising generic and competency-based questions is important as it gives you time to prepare for potential questions. Of course, these specific questions may not arise but just going through the process will help considerably.

Visual Communication

Whether you are attending an interview with a company which has an informal clothing policy or whether you need to be 'suited and booted', you need to ensure you look the best you can. If you don't know the company's dress policy you should go 'suited and booted'. Remember, first impressions count. Also, looking your best helps to boost general confidence and demonstrates that you are serious about the opportunity.

Body Language

Have you ever tried to explain something to someone when they are sitting with their arms folded tightly, with their legs crossed and wondered why you are struggling to get your point across? This is a typical example of someone who is just not prepared to listen at that time.

You don't need to be an expert but an understanding of basic body language may help you during an interview. In fact, you may find the interviewer is applying it by mirroring your actions, such as leaning back or forwards in the chair, touching spectacles or rubbing their forehead. Fascinating!

Eye contact, firm handshake, enthusiastic hand gestures, smiling and nodding when in agreement should all create a good impression and be the start of rapport building.

Targeting Your Job Search

There are only benefits to taking a targeted approach to job searching. The more focused you can be regarding your future job role the more likely you are to achieve it.

Many people take the shotgun approach by focusing on 'quantity' rather than 'quality' when sending out their CV and wonder why they have a high rejection rate.

By following the previous tips regarding CV writing, you should have created a concise document which shows evidence of your suitability for a role. All that effort will be wasted if it is sent out to irrelevant companies.

A targeted job search should make looking for your next job less of an ordeal as you will be identifying companies that can meet your current and future needs and is more likely to create excitement rather than fear.

These needs will not only concern your job skills and knowledge but must also cover 'personal'. Many hours are spent in the workplace so it is important to get as close a fit to your personality and cultural needs as possible.

Identifying your Strengths

'Strengths' in this context relate to natural talents. There is significant evidence that when people are able to apply their natural talents at work then they are enthusiastic and highly motivated to achieve their best performance. This makes it an excellent starting point for a targeted job search.

Sometimes people are on automatic pilot in a role, going through the motions and are not consciously considering if they are enjoying what they are doing. When they leave and look for other roles they often continue doing the same job with another employer. This may well be the best choice but it makes sense to consider other options. If someone has been made redundant after a few years with an employer, they may feel a lack of confidence when job searching because they feel out of their comfort zone. Essentially, they feel this way as their identity is intrinsically linked to their last job. Identifying Strengths can create greater awareness of what they really enjoy and how they can apply transferable skills.

I am accredited in the Strengthscope ™ assessment tool that provides a comprehensive measurement of your strengths and the extent to which these are applied, or have been applied, at work. Through discussion, you will have more information regarding distinctive strengths - or 'significant seven' – and how you can maximise these at work. A strengths-based approach does not ignore 'weaknesses' but discussion is around how these can be managed whilst remaining focused on Strengths.

- Think about a project or task at work where you felt highly motivated and enthusiastic.
- What were you doing?
- What strengths were you using?

If you do not want to have an assessment of this type, it is still worth thinking hard about what you **consider** to be your strengths at work as a starting point. **Examples:** Developing Others, Courage, Efficiency, Empathy

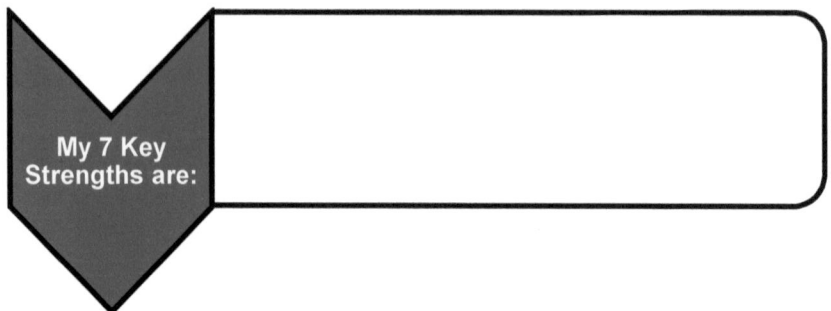

If you are interested in learning more about the online Strengthscope™ assessment, please contact me at **marilyn@careerlifestylechoices.com**

Identifying your Personal Values

In the words of Mahatma Ghandi:

"Your beliefs become your thoughts. Your thoughts become your words. Your words become your actions. Your actions become your habits. Your habits become your values. Your values become your destiny".

We are now living at a time where life expectancy to 100 years is not considered to be unusual and retirement age is rising. People are generally becoming more health conscious and if they are going to work longer, many are looking at a better work / life balance.

Personal Values are what you consider important in life and, therefore, tend to influence attitude and behaviour. I support the view that if the work that you do reflects your values then you are more likely to be engaged, motivated and true to yourself. You will be generating a 'feel good' persona which is great for you and the people with whom you work.

Taking the Fear Out of Interviews

When personal values are aligned with your business choices then you are thought to be living your life to your fullest. To get the best out of your values, I recommend that you look at them weekly. If you are living your values - great! If not, and as values are generally positive and worthy, try to develop habits or create situations where you are using them.

<u>Just a few examples of Values:</u>

Accountability
Appreciation
Being the best you can be
Commitment
Family
Fun
Gratitude
Helping others
Honesty
Integrity

Love
Loyalty
Not wasting time
Patience
Reliability
Resilience
Respecting cultural differences
Responsibility
Self-discipline
Willingness

- Take an hour to think about your values and why they are important to you.
- Extensive lists of personal values can be obtained by a Google search.
- Think about those that are serving you well. Make a list of values relevant to you and select the Top 10
- Think about other criteria which you consider to be important in your next role e.g location, working hours etc

My Top 10 Values:

Other Key Criteria

Identifying your Skills and Achievements

Whilst Skills and Achievements are on your CV, it is worthwhile to look at them closely and identify those which could be transferable across different roles and industries. Consider the Achievements which you enjoyed best and think about the Strengths and Competencies you were applying. Also think about the

Write a list of the skills you:

- Wish to use
- Don't wish to use
- Wish to develop
- Consider are transferable across different industries

Taking the Fear Out of Interviews

aspects of the role which you did NOT enjoy. Sometimes, it is helpful to get honest feedback and a fresh perspective from a friend or colleague.

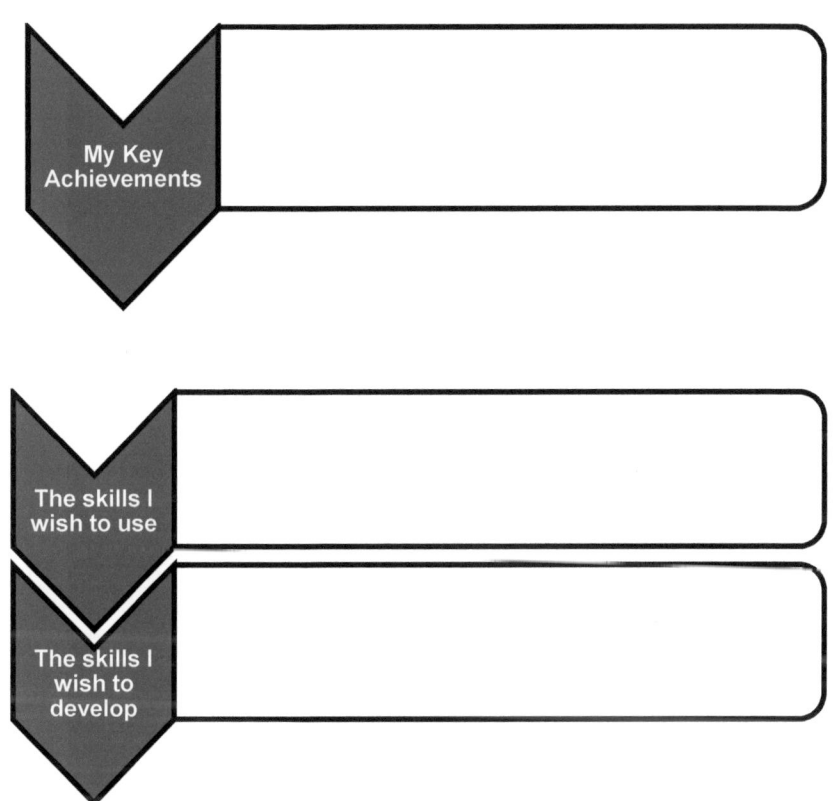

Identifying Potential Roles and Companies

So to this point, you should have far more clarity around your 'needs' and 'wants'.

<u>For example:</u>

My 7 Key Strengths	• Collaboration, Compassion • Courage, Developing Others • Enthusiasm, Flexibilty • Self-improvement
My Top 10 Values	• Achievement, Belonging, Contribution • Diversity, Fairness, Family, Independence • Being the best I can be, Teamwork • Making the best of time
Other Key Criteria	• To reduce commuting time • To work in a growth industry
Skills I wish to use	• Leadership, Relationship Management • Problem Solving, Budget Planning • Retail industry experience
Skills I wish to develop	• Presentations to groups • Report writing • Event Management • Business Development

Taking the Fear Out of Interviews

Next steps >

1. Research Recruitment Agencies
- Identify those which specialise in your sector. These are really extensive covering all industries including General Clerical, IT, HR, Marketing, Retail, Finance, Engineering, Public Sector and Niche providers - to name but a few!

2. Research Advertised Roles
- Search Companies and Recruitment Agencies vacancy lists online to see which fit *your* selection criteria
- The internet is the best route but if you do not have access then most libraries have the facility or ask friends. Check local papers.

Then decide >

Job Roles which appeal to me

Industries & Companies which appeal to me

Getting into Action

By this stage you should be clear about the type of job role you are seeking and familiar with the application and interview process. Now is the time to put everything into action! Knowledge without action obviously won't get you very far towards achieving your goal of finding the best job for you.

Have a Goal

It is widely accepted that having a goal helps us to focus and focus is what we need to achieve our goals - but it starts with a goal! There are many goal-setting techniques but I have found that the **S.M.A.R.T** method works well. In this way your goals are **Specific, Measurable, Achievable, Realistic and Time-lined**.

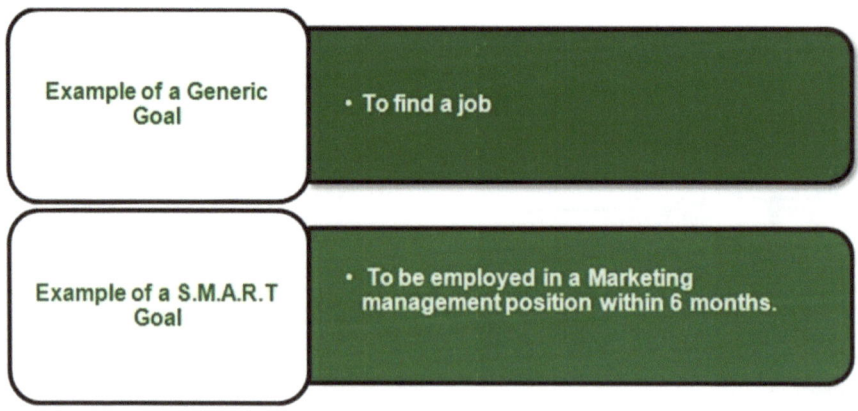

Treat your Job Search like a Project

This approach helps to create focus and disciplined daily habits. It is much more effective to have consistent activity rather than stop and start where it is easy to lose momentum. Every project has Threshold or Milestone points, so it helps to create an overview of them for the total duration of your job search timeline. I think it works well to start with your goal and timeline and fill in the steps that lead to it.

Let's take the above goal as an example:

Activity	Months					
	1	2	3	4	5	6
Goal: To be employed in a marketing management position within 6 months						
Receive Job offer						
Attend interviews with companies						
Attend interviews with agencies						
Send out CV to companies and agencies						
Research target companies						
Identify work and lifestyle needs						

You can see from this overview that researching, sending out CVs and attending interviews are continuous actions to give you greatest chance of success. The next step breaks down this overview into weekly activity where you should set yourself daily targets. If you review your activity on a weekly basis and then set the activity for the following week, it helps to keep you focused, energised and motivated to achieve the outcome. Throughout this process you will be receiving feedback from agencies and companies and you may find that your initial direction changes.

Example of a Weekly Activity Plan

Weekly Activity	M	T	W	Th	F	S	S
Research at least 20 companies							
Send out CV to at least 10 companies							
Research job fairs							
Research agencies and select 3							
Arrange meeting with selected agencies							
Network on Linkedin, Facebook and Twitter							
Personal Development - practise interview questions							
Review activity and plan next week							
Time with family and friends							

Actual activity should be driven by the level of competition in your chosen industry sector and the availability of roles. You can see, however, the principles of this Weekly Plan is a little and often. If you do something every day it should help your mind to be focused on the goal. In this example, I have not put any project activity on the Sunday because it helps to have a day of rest which, in my experience, clears the head and means that you look forward to the next day's activity. Obviously you will need to adjust activity to suit your personal and cultural needs.

Be your Own Boss until you find another one

Sometimes this is difficult because you need to be brutally honest with yourself. Until you find the career of your choice, you are looking at your boss when you look in the mirror. Treating your job search as a project helps to create this mindset and should encourage you to review your activity and results on a daily and weekly basis.

Plans should always be 'tweaked' to keep you on the right track to reach your goal. The road you thought you would take at the beginning is likely to change due to life circumstances and what you learn along the way. Most managers in the workplace will be looking at the results of their team's efforts and making necessary changes. As you are now 'your own boss' you need to do the same until you find your career or job of choice. If you, for instance, have not achieved your weekly activity, ask yourself the big question "Why Not?" and be honest with yourself.

If you have not kept up with the planned activity because you have been distracted, or have been disorganised or just had a bad week, then realise that this is absolutely normal but try not to have these weeks too often! We all know that every action has a consequence so the more positive actions we can take, the better.

Making Friends with the Agencies

Professional recruitment consultants can be your greatest asset so here are a few tips regarding how to help them work best on your behalf.

Choose 3 agencies with good reputations. The recruitment industry is highly competitive and recruitment consultants will be less motivated to be pro-active on your behalf if you are registered with too many agencies. This is why I recommend that you do your research and identify three, with good reputations, in your market sector. There are hundreds to choose from in general and specialist areas such as IT, Finance, Marketing, Sales, Clerical, Engineering and niche players- the choice is vast. Sources for these would be the internet, local papers, specialist magazines and libraries.

The best source, however, are referrals. If an agency is recommended to you then the consultant is more likely to meet with you.

Contact your selected agencies before sending your CV to confirm that they should be able to help you. They are likely to want to see your CV first but ask them if you can have an interview with them as soon as possible. Putting a 'face to a name' has obvious benefits.

Agree with the Recruitment Consultant how often you should keep in touch. Following up from any interview or meeting is important but if it is too regular it can have a de-motivating affect. I suggest once a week unless agreed otherwise.

Ask for feedback on your CV, if one of your selected agencies does not invite you for interview and use this information to select another one.

Listen to the agency's advice - they can be a torrent of information which you can channel into finding your career goal.

Feedback to your Recruitment Consultant following interviews. Whether it is positive or negative it will help them fine-tune their search

Get post-interview feedback from the Recruitment Consultant so that you can apply it to your next interview. Be open to any constructive criticism.

Be available so that the Recruitment Consultant can contact you at any time.

Move on if a Recruitment Consultant lacks empathy, does not feedback constructively or cannot show you the activity they have done on your behalf. Some Recruitment Consultants are more professional than others.

Speculative Approaches

Sometimes people make the mistake of taking the 'shotgun' approach by sending out CVs on a speculative basis to companies in their sector.

This is not a good idea because:

> The recipient will know that it is a speculative approach and will think they are just one of a number.

> They will gain the impression that you have not thought seriously about your suitability for a role.

> Contacts in companies change and there is nothing worse than receiving an email, letter or CV addressed to the wrong person. Again, it will show that you have not given your application much thought.

> You are basically creating spam mail for their inbox or in-tray which won't be appreciated.

Networking

The value of networking is that you are meeting people face to face and can quickly establish rapport. There are numerous opportunities to network either informally or formally.

For instance, if your sector is 'marketing' then there will be specialist networking groups either at a physical location or online. Online is an excellent first step as there may not be networking groups in your local area.

Search social media, such as LinkedIn, Facebook, Twitter and establish contact with people in your job roles, industry sectors or other relevant professional groups. Your aim is to open conversation and not 'sell yourself' hard.

Job Fairs offer an excellent opportunity to meet companies and recruitment agencies in a relatively informal setting. Search the internet for national events and local events. Attending Trade Fairs provides the opportunity to learn more about companies in your industry, to engage in conversation with company representatives, to create that all important first impression and to learn about future job opportunities if they are not recruiting at that time. They also enable you to judge competing companies in a market sector which all helps with your decision making. These are also advertised extensively on the internet but check for local events via such sources as the Chamber of Commerce.

Job Application Letters and Emails

Sometimes people submit an excellent CV but let themselves down with a poorly thought-out application letter. This is another instance where you are judged on your ability to communicate well in writing. If the company is not impressed at this stage then you may well have a more testing time at interview. If it is particularly bad, then you may not even reach interview stage as good communication is a universal requirement these days.

<u>Here are a few tips:</u>

Read the text of the advertisement and make a note of the prominent words and qualities which are being sought.

Structure the letter in this way (See an example on next page)

> a. Confirm the role, where you saw it advertised and any reference numbers. Get their interest by repeating key phrases or words from the advertisement.
>
> b. Highlight where your experience is a really good fit for the role
>
> c. Finish with a closing statement which should include your request to go forward to the next stage.

Don't be too familiar when addressing the contact. Whether you are applying by email or letter, use Mr, Mrs, Ms in the first instance.

Kind regards, Best regards, Regards, Yours sincerely are all accepted ways to sign off for letters or emails.

Marilyn Black

Example / Job Application Letter:

Dear

Marketing Manager. Ref 1234 (put this in the subject line if sending an email)

In response to your advertisement in the Guardian for a Marketing Manager with event management and team leadership skills, I am enclosing my CV for your consideration.

In particular, I would like to draw your attention to the fact that I have:

- Organised medium and large national events within the retail industry.
- Have a post-graduate diploma in Event Management.
- Led a team of six across all marketing disciplines, including online marketing

XYZ has an excellent reputation and I would be very interested in meeting you to discuss my experience further.

I look forward to hearing from you.

Kind regards

What You Can Legally Expect

Employment Law and other codes of conduct safeguard the interests of people in the workplace. They cover the whole spectrum of employment but I am just highlighting information that is relevant to Recruitment & Selection.

Employment Law Discriminations

It is against the Law for interviewers to discriminate against someone on the grounds of:

- Age
- Colour
- Disability
- Ethnic background
- Gender
- Gender reassignment

- Marital status
- Nationality
- Religion or belief / or lack of Race
- Pregnancy/ Maternity Leave
- Sexual orientation

More information can be seen at:
www.gov.uk/discrimination-your-rights

Information Commissioner's Office (ICO)

The ICO helps employers comply with best practices regarding Data Protection. You should be aware that:

Companies can verify that the details you have stated on your CV are correct but must inform you of what will be checked and how it will be done. For example, checking qualifications or by taking up references.

If you are seeking employment in a high risk area, then **an employer can check with the Criminal Records Bureau.**

A company needs to inform you of any verification process as soon as it is reasonably practicable. You should then be informed of any discrepancies and have the opportunity to address them.

When applying to a job advertisement, you should be informed of the name of the company.

Recruitment Agencies should identify themselves in an advertisement and inform you if your information is likely to be used for any purpose of which you are unaware.

Agencies should inform you of any company which holds your information.

Companies and Agencies must handle your personal information with respect.

Sometimes employers do not wish to be named early in the recruitment process. **In this case, the agency should only send them anonymous information about your application.** You should be informed of the employer's name if your application is taken further.

Your CV and related documentation should be stored securely by the agency or company and should not be kept longer than necessary. They should then be destroyed securely.

You have **the right to request information** recorded about you at interview. Companies should have a process in place for this eventuality.

More information can be seen at: **https://ico.org.uk/**

Let's Practise

Competency-based Interview Questions

When answering a competency-based question, a very straightforward way to ensure you have answered fully, is the **STAR** method.

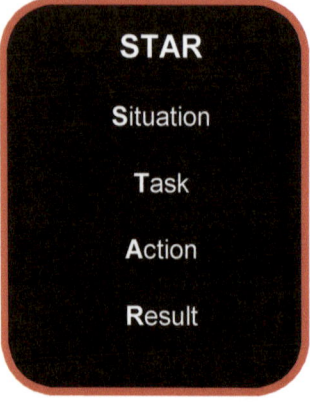

There are no standard competency-based interview questions but these will give you some idea of what to expect

In the following example you can see how it can work..

| Sample Question | Please give me an example when you have used your initiative at work. |

(Sometimes competency-based questions are not technically questions but statements. This is because the interviewer needs to ask an 'open' question which encourages a fuller response. If it was rephrased as "Can you give me an example…" then a candidate could just say "Yes" or "No")

Taking the Fear Out of Interviews

A response using the STAR technique:

"At the time I was leading a customer service team **(Situation)** when I was asked to resolve a difficult issue with one of our regular customers who had complained. **(Task).**

(Actions) First, I spoke with the customer to understand the problem more fully. He was upset due to goods not being delivered and I promised to organise a fresh delivery whilst looking into the cause. He wanted assurances that this situation would not happen again and I said it would be a top priority for me to find a resolution.

The goods had left our depot on time but the driver became ill and was taken to hospital. He had not been able to call the depot or the customer as everything happened very quickly.

I spoke again to the customer to say that another delivery was on its way. My company needed to change and build in safeguards to the process so that this problem could not arise again. I suggested that an alarm system should be installed in the delivery vans which the driver could press in the event of any delay. One press would be for up to 30 minutes delay, pressing the alarm twice would mean 30 minutes - 1 hour delay and three presses would alert the company to a longer timeframe or an emergency. The company would contact the customer to make them aware of any delays. This system was far safer and quicker than the drivers calling in on mobile phones.

(Result) The customer was satisfied and has given us more business because we acted quickly and the company can now guarantee an efficient delivery service. Our drivers were also pleased because they had found that reliance on mobile phones had caused safety challenges and communication was *not guaranteed due to signal loss in some locations. I was given recognition at the company end of year event for remaining calm in a difficult situation and creating a very cost effective system which ultimately increased sales."*

The above example is to demonstrate the structure of an answer, your initial response may not be as detailed. Respond as fully as you can and the interviewer will continue to ask questions until they are satisfied with the answer. This is not, however, an interrogation and if you relax and treat it like a normal conversation then you will find it easier.

Also an interviewer will always be conscious of assessing responses with regard to other competencies in their selection criteria. For instance, whilst the above example is an 'initiative' question, from this response the interviewer could gain insight Problem Solving, Relationship Management and Communication.

<u>Practise answering the following questions the S.T.A.R way:</u>

Achieving Results

Competency Description:

Delivers expected results in a timely manner

> **Question:** *Describe a time when you set and achieved a goal.*

Situation / Task

Action Taken

Result

Marilyn Black

Attention to Detail

Competency Description:

Applies thoroughness to all aspects of work performed.

> **Question**: *Give me a specific example of a time when you were working on something very important. How did you ensure nothing was overlooked?*

Situation / Task

Action Taken

Result

Communicating

Competency Description:

Represents ideas and thoughts in a clear, focused manner using effective verbal and non-verbal communication techniques in both formal and informal settings.

> **Question:** *When, over the last six months, would you say your communication skills have been most affective?*

Situation / Task

Action Taken

Result

Marilyn Black

Decision Making & Judgement

Competency Description:

Reaches appropriate conclusions and takes sensible action on the basis of thorough analysis and past experience

> **Question**: *What has been the most difficult decision you have made in a working environment*

Situation / Task

Action Taken

Result

Flexibility

Competency Description:

Does what is necessary, even if it doesn't fit with own needs or ideas

> **Question:** *Please give me an example when work priorities have changed at short notice......How did you deal with this?*

Situation / Task

Action Taken

Result

Marilyn Black

Influencing

Competency Description:

Demonstrated the ability to present ideas persuasively to provide insight, gain buy-in and or steer others to specific outcomes.

> **Question:** *When was the last time you persuaded somebody, or a group, to do something they clearly did not want to do?*

Situation / Task

Action Taken

Result

Initiative

Competency Description:

Takes a pro-active, self-reliant approach, identifying and seizing opportunities, taking decisive action.

> **Question**: *Please give me an example when you achieved an objective under pressure. What were the key problems you encountered? How did you overcome them?*

Situation / Task

Action Taken

Result

Marilyn Black

Problem Solving

Competency Description:

Identifies root-cause of problems, generates options and delivers optimum solution.

> **Question:** *Describe a situation where the cause of a problem was not initially clear?*

Situation / Task

Action Taken

Result

Resilience

Competency Description:

Demonstrates the ability to recover strength, fortitude and motivation quickly in the face of adversity.

> **Question:** *Please give me an example when you have not achieved an objective at the first attempt?*

Situation / Task

Action Taken

Result

Marilyn Black

Teamwork

Competency Description:

Works effectively in collaboration with others, encouraging others to express ideas and opinions

> **Question:** *Please give me an example when you were particularly supportive to others*

Situation / Task

Action Taken

Result

Time Management

Competency Description:

Planning and exercising conscious control over the amount of time spent on specific activities to increase efficiency and productivity

> **Question:** *Give me an example when you have had to manage several tasks at the same time*

Situation / Task

Action Taken

Result

Thank You

A huge "Thank You" for taking the time to read this book and I really hope you have enjoyed it and will benefit from it.

The recruitment marketplace is continually evolving but these practices have stood the test of time. Obviously, it is important to be constantly aware of fresh developments and approaches, such as using Social Media, and I will continue to explore what is working well or not.

I do offer 121 Interview coaching. so if you would like more personal assistance, please email me at **marilyn@careerlifestylechoices.com** .

Hopefully, I have succeeded in creating a comprehensive guide to increasing your effectiveness at interviews and overcoming other career challenges you may have experienced - but, if you need clarity on anything, please contact me.

Here's to your great success!

All the best

Marilyn

www.ingramcontent.com/pod-product-compliance
Lightning Source LLC
Chambersburg PA
CBHW040836180526
45159CB00001B/210